Why I Wag My Tail

Shannea L. Patterson

Contents

There are a few people in my life who have encouraged me in ways that bring tears to my eyes when I think about the support and love they've extended. Self-esteem is important; so is having someone who believes in you.

Phyllis, you were there at one of life's tipping points; you were instrumental in my life tipping in a positive direction. Thank you!

All my friends, you are my family, and I love you for that. A special thanks to all of you who supported my focus group, read drafts, and shared your feedback.☺

Disclaimer
This book is based on my interpretation of events in my life. Some events are taken out of sequence, and some experiences omitted, in an effort to summarize. Some names have been changed or omitted.

Introduction

After ten years of self-employment in the childcare industry, I closed my business and began re-acclimating myself into corporate America. Within five or six years, I worked with over fifteen different companies, sometimes leaving by choice, sometimes not.

Growing up I was taught good work ethics: you show up on time or early, find out what is expected and exceed expectations, and you come to work every day unless you absolutely, unavoidably can't. I'm talking, "I'm having surgery today" or a bone is broken, can't go to work. Slight fever, headache, cramps—any of that,

I'm there! One of my first serious jobs after high school was with the United States Postal Service. I started off in a large group of temporary seasonal workers knowing only a small group would be recommended to stay past the holiday rush. After making that first cut I was promoted to a different class of temporary worker, still with the understanding that any day could be my last day. The day I was selected to stay on and promoted once again, I was at work on a summer day with three layers of clothes on, fighting a 102 degree fever – still present at work.

I thought a good work ethic and an aptitude to learn things quickly were the essential ingredients to a recipe for success. Not only did I do well in self-employment, but from an employer's perspective I thought a company would kill to have an employee like me.

Corporate America can be a "dog eat dog" world, and I walked right in wearing milk bone underwear. To say I was naive would be an understatement. I had this huge sense of right and wrong, and fairness. I was certain any good company, or good person, would share the same preoccupation.

Why I Wag My Tail is a short motivational story of my journey integrating into the corporate world, and how my experience affected my personal and professional life. While the journey started off pretty rough, I eventually found my way to a smoother path, allowing for optimal life experiences and the opportunity to live the life I wanted to live, instead of dreaming about it. I went from struggling spiritually, emotionally, financially, and directionally, to spiritual and emotional peace, knowing my purpose, and more than doubling my income in a short period of time.

If I could have learned some of the things I know now and gotten the chip off my shoulder earlier in life, I'm certain it would have been a huge benefit, saving myself a lot of anger and pain. My hope is that you connect with my experiences to define or redefine what success is *for you,* and make choices and live a life that supports your objectives so that you authentically and effortlessly *wag your tail!*

Chapter 1
The Dog Analogy

Conversation with Frank

In response to a conflict at work, I asked my friend Frank, "Your personality is just as aggressive or as intimidating as mine, if not more. How are you able to get along and do so well at work and I'm struggling?

Frank started laughing and asked, "Why?"

I said, "Well, the woman who fired me said she was intimidated by me. She said I did great work, was always on time, but she claimed to be intimidated by me. She couldn't articulate anything I had done or anything to substantiate her feelings; just that she was intimidated. She said I don't joke with her. I don't get how that plays into intimidation. I've never had a confrontation with the woman, never raised my voice, and she never saw me angry, so I don't understand. Not only am I barely 5'3", but I also rarely gave the woman the time of day, so I don't understand how she could claim to be intimidated—let alone why the company would support her and let that play out as a reason to fire me."

Frank started cracking up. I mean, laughing like what I just said was knee-slapping funny. Now, I've put a little soul into my story, and I'm as serious as a heart attack, so I'm sooooo not feeling him laughing.

Then he asked me a question: "Are you afraid of dogs?"

"What?"

Frank, with more laughter: "Are you afraid of dogs?"

"I don't want to talk about dogs right now. I'm trying to ask you a serious question and get some perspective about what is happening to me."

Frank tried to stop laughing, because he saw I was getting irritated, but he couldn't stop. He managed to spit out, "Okay, okay! Just answer the question: are you afraid of dogs?"

"I don't know! It depends! Big dog? Little dog? What is the dog doing? Is the dog growling and showing its teeth, or is it wagging its tail? It just depends!"

At this point Frank was literally bent over, hand grasping his side, cracking up laughing. Not only was I not laughing, but I didn't see what was so funny. He was laughing like I had just tested out a bit in my comedy routine.

Normally, Frank is direct and focused. I was looking at him *not* answering my question, and all I could think was, "What the hell?" I was as hot as fish grease, but I couldn't help but smile a little bit. When you see someone laughing that hard you can't help but break a little, even if you know they are laughing *at* you and not *with* you.

I asked, "What is so funny? How is it that I ask you a question about how you are successful and I'm not, and you respond with hysterical laughter and a question about dogs?"

Frank is a Brown man in his mid 50's; he looks like Eddie Murphy with a confidence and walk that resembles Denzel Washington's swagger. Frank has led a full life, from hustling in the streets, to owning and operating a multi-million dollar company, with experiences and relationships with people from all different walks of life. Frank has a strong energy and presence, and definitely marches to the beat of a different drummer—a strong confident march I might add. He can swing from social and engaging to alone in a room full of people in a matter of seconds. If there was anyone I felt comfortable asking how to get along, it was Frank.

Frank finally answered, "Okay. Unfortunately, for some people, when they see a black person they see a dog. The same way you feel whether or not you are afraid of a dog depends on what the dog is doing and all of the other variables you described, that is how some people respond to black people."

He continued, "The same way you would stop to watch the dog for signs that it is okay or try to figure out what's up with the dog, that is the very thing that is happening to you. People are waiting to know if you are a friendly dog or not. When you can't figure out where the intimidation or negative energy is coming from, it is simply because they see you as a dog, and most importantly, a dog that *isn't* wagging its tail."

I responded, "Wait a second! Why should I have to wag my tail or do anything else to prove I'm okay? I might not be wagging my tail, but I'm not growling either. I'm just minding my own business trying to do the job I was hired to do. If I make friends along the way, great, but if not, that is fine too; and I shouldn't have to be preoccupied with wagging my tail trying to prove to anyone that 'I'm a friendly Negro!' If I am a dog, I'm just a dog minding my own business walking down the street, not wagging my tail, but not growling either."

"Well, that might be how you feel as the dog that is minding its own business, but that might not be the perception of the person who is petrified of a dog. And you are absolutely right. You shouldn't have to wag your tail or do anything else to prove yourself friendly, and you don't. You don't have to do anything, Shannea. You don't even have to wake up tomorrow morning if you don't want to. But you asked me how I get along so well and you don't; it's because I choose to wag my tail."

Schmuck! (That part is only said in my head—remember I mentioned Frank is pretty intimidating himself!) "Then what is the alternative?" I said.

"Keep doing what you are doing and having the same experiences and outcomes, or make different choices for different results. You can be right and unemployed, or you can make some changes in an effort to be successful."

I would later have more questions, but in that moment I just sat there trying to digest what Frank had said to me. That conversation was something I will never forget, and an analogy I have used for myself over and over again in both my personal and professional life. When I see a pit bull walking down the street, as soon as I come out from hiding behind a tree, my car, or the safety of my gate, I start cracking up reflecting on what Frank was trying to get me to see about people's reaction to me. Maybe that is why Frank found my question so funny. Even though I couldn't see the parallel, I'm sure Frank intuitively understood, right or wrong, the reaction some people had to me. I know of pit bulls that wouldn't hurt a fly, and equally, I've seen the horror stories broadcast on television. So my gut reaction from the negative stereotype of a pit bull is to hide or seek safety first, and find out the facts later; this despite what I know to be true about some very user friendly pit bulls. Again, right or wrong, my initial reaction is based on the reputation and the look of pit bulls.

What is funny is that I would not classify myself as someone who is afraid of dogs, just like I know several people who abuse power and position that "know not what I speak" when I talk about adverse treatment people sometimes receive due to racism and prejudice. Just as I can't imagine why someone would be afraid of, or intimidated by, a 5'3", big boned (it's just water weight, just water weight y'all), Brown woman without specific reason or without really knowing me, I'm sure the friendly dog who just wants to have a sniff and greet can't understand why I'm in a corner shaking, yelling profanities at his master, or trying to find the number to the dog catcher.

Now let me explain my use of the word "Brown" woman. I am what some call African American or Black, but I prefer to use the term Brown. I had one of those "ah ha" moments while I was a day care provider in a conversation with my four year old cousin who felt it appropriate to say negatively "with your black self" to someone because she was much lighter than they were. In using that moment to increase her awareness I was explaining to her how we are all different shades of black, and my own thought process and the literal side of me was challenged. In using both our arms as an example, it was apparent different shades of brown was much more accurate.

I'd also like to clarify that I definitely don't see myself, or any other race for that matter, as a dog or anything less than human, so please don't get your undies in a bunch over the reference. Analogies work very well for me and I use them in most of my conversations— the conversations I have in my head as well as with other humans. Analogies allow me to remove myself or the personal aspects from the scenario in an effort to gain some objectivity and perspective; I think objectivity is paramount when you want to look at a situation and gain more than your initial lens might offer.

When Frank took my question and answered in a context I could relate to, my thought process was open with no defense. Since we were talking about dogs, there wasn't much I was interested in defending. I'm a very direct person and I find analogies allow me to shoot with the intensity I enjoy in conversation without a person feeling attacked. The objective in this analogy, and any other analogy I use, is to center on the big picture—not the "you" or the "me,"—and consider another perspective.

The conversation with Frank was definitely what I would consider a pivotal point in my journey. I went from making over five thousand dollars per month self employed, at a time when that was considered "good money," to less than half of what I was accustomed to making, with breaks of unemployment every so often while trying to find my way in corporate America. I struggled and banged my head against walls, sometimes the same wall, until I had a shift in my attitude and my approach to life. Once I created an opening and embraced this pivotal moment with Frank, everything began to change, both professionally and personally. In a few years' time, I more than doubled my income and began having the most incredible and powerful interactions with my universe. I transitioned from a person fighting for survival, to a successful positive contributor in my world—successful in my career and doing okay financially, but most importantly, successful internally within my soul, spirit and being.

That is a gloss over to the end, but let me tell you about the middle! Before the better me won me over, there were some kick-butt, drag-out internal arguments. Internal conflict is a beast!

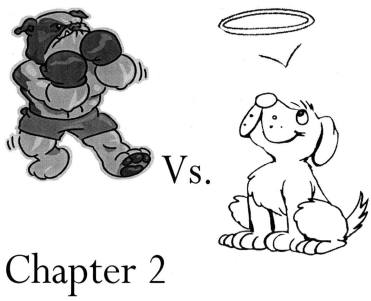

Vs.

Chapter 2
Internal Conflict

Right vs. successful

The conversation with Frank finally gave me some information to help me understand some of my experiences and how things could go from sugar to shit in a matter of seconds, but I was still conflicted. I had a better understanding about what had happened with some of my past experiences, but I was stuck in kiddy-land attached to "But it's not fair!" and "I shouldn't have to!" Without realizing it, I had my own sense of entitlement. I felt I was entitled to a certain life experience and promise, of fair and equitable treatment and opportunity. I also felt I was entitled to do my job without any responsibility to attend to the social wants of my team—to be left alone! I thought about the end of my conversation with Frank where he so kindly reminded me that I didn't have to do anything, but deep down I knew something needed to change if I wanted to get myself out of that perpetual cycle of madness with work and work relationships.

I was going back and forth in my head. In one moment, I was motivated, and clapped my hands together in that "on your mark, get ready, go" sense, and told myself that I had a plan—I was going to figure out how to wag my tail! In the next moment, I was standing, flexed, forehead furrowed saying, "Forget that! I'm not selling out and working to change myself to make other people feel comfortable. Instead of wagging my tail all over the place all the doggone time, I'll just find some people who aren't afraid of dogs!"

I wanted to talk about it, debate about it, pretty much throw a tantrum about it, as if getting people to validate my feelings and my experiences would somehow miraculously create a change in my experiences and prove Frank wrong. I wanted to call Frank and have another round of the same argument, but I knew there was nothing new that would be said. Frank's bottom line was *if* you don't want people to be intimidated, then show yourself friendly—wag that tail, crazy lady! And if you don't choose to do that, fine, but shut it; stop the whining! Frank has a saying: "If you choose to walk in the water, don't complain about being wet."

Despite knowing how Frank would respond, I wanted to argue with him. I wanted to defend my view of the injustice of racism, the abuse of power and privilege, and the thought that having to work harder to get an equal playing field was foul. I wanted some validation.

I had a host of other people I could have called who would have given me the "Yeah! You're right! You're right! I wouldn't wag my tail either," endorsement, but I wanted *him* to concede. I wanted Frank to agree with me and then give me some magic beans or a secret recipe to cure my woes, start a revolution, or give me some other spiritual soliloquy about how Brown people have made it through. I was having a hard time with the thought of my whole situation, my victim stance, being minimized to a mere matter of choice—my choice.

Have you ever listened to someone complain endlessly about a choice they made, or, even worse, a choice they were excited about once upon a time? People who are married—and we don't have a lot of arranged marriages in the U.S.—but don't want to get a divorce, and complain on end about how miserable they are because of "her" and how the marriage is a dead end street? Or a person who has worked for the same company for twenty years, has nothing good to say about the company, but they have no intention of finding a new job? That is being a victim of your life, a victim of your choices—self-inflicted pain. Don't get me wrong: there are definitely times, past and present, where people have dealt with situations where choice was minimal, or they had to make tough choices: worship your way and die, or deny your religion and live; slavery or a beating/death; the Holocaust; fight in a war or lose your freedom—the list goes on and on. I'm just stating what I hope is becoming obvious: this wasn't one of those times! The thing of it is, when you are smack dab in the middle of your madness, it is hard to be humble and focused enough to have an Urkel (from the TV show *Family Matters*) "Did I do that?" moment. Who wants to take responsibility for messing their own stuff up?

About one year before my dog analogy conversation with Frank, I was in a recruit class to become a volunteer firefighter for the Auburn Mountain View Fire Department. On my first day as a recruit my chief addressed the class. One of the first things he mentioned was this: "...and I don't want to hear anything about the word *fair* while you are in this class. *Fair* is something that comes to your local county once or twice a year for you to ride rides, play games, and be amused. Outside of that, there is no such word in this world, which is my world."

Good googlie-woo! There I was, having a real live experience with someone telling me that I could check fairness at the door! There were no "should be, supposed to be" rules—what he said went! We're talking about a lot more than wagging a tail here. What do you do when someone tells you directly to your face that your whole premise of life—justice, equality, and fairness—just ain't so? Justice just ain't happening, and no one cares! It's funny that I had been arguing that life wasn't fair and experiences are tainted and directed by those in power and position, but I still had shock waves strong enough to give a cold fish the warm and fuzzies when someone stared me right in my face and said, "Oh yeah! Life is not fair lady, and we are telling you straight up, no ifs ands or buts about it."

What do you do when you want to achieve something that is held by a person who says 'you can have this if you play by my rules and my rules aren't fair?' Well...you decide. If you want it, and success means getting it, then you make choices that support getting it and being successful. If whatever it takes causes you to lose your integrity, and if having integrity is part of what success means for you, then you are still successful in choosing to stand your ground and stand up for what you believe in.

Even though the conversation with Frank came a year after the recruit experience, and the chief was addressing everyone in a general sense, where Frank's message was close and personal, it was the same message with a much more aggressive tone. I can be right and unemployed. I can be right and not a firefighter. Whatever the issue is, I can spend time debating about the right and wrong, or I can get satisfied and have acceptance with the conditions of satisfaction and terms for success. I can stop using my energy negatively by resisting, and accept what is so and figure out what I'm going to do to change it.

I had one job experience where my supervisor had some real life dementia issues, actual medical diagnosis, but her boss wasn't aware of her mental condition. You could say "123" and the supervisor would hear "AB" and forget to add a "C." She literally wrote notes on her computer about where she placed her lunch or where she parked her car. We were in several meetings where she would either delete or distort 60% of the information.

I complained to Frank. This was a while after our initial "wag your tail" conversation, and I think Frank was getting fed up with my slow pace of processing how much control I had over my life and my experiences. I was laying into Frank about how crazy the supervisor was and how oppressed I was, and Frank said something along the lines of, "Well, what are you going to do about it?"

I said, "I can't do anything! I can't even have a conversation about it if afterwards she isn't going to remember the conversation!"

Frank said, "Okay. So what is your exit strategy?"

Silence. "Well, I don't know."

From Frank: "If it is as bad as you say it is, you really have two choices. Either do something about it or quit."

"But I can't quit."

"Why?"

"Because I have to pay my mortgage, pay my bills and take care of myself."

"You have to or you choose to?"

"I have to! No one is going to do it for me. I'm the only person I can depend on."

Frank: "I see what you are saying about paying your mortgage and supporting yourself, but that seems like a choice."

"No, it isn't a choice, I have to."

"Or what?"

Silence. "Or I would lose everything I've worked so hard for."

Frank said, "So, you choose to work in a situation you are unhappy with to keep your house and to be able to pay your bills?"

Shoot! I'm frustrated again.

Frank says, "All I'm saying, Shannea, is that we all make choices for different reasons. But if you choose to walk in the water, for whatever reason, don't make the rest of us pay the price for your choices. If you need to make a new choice, then do that."

"Okay. Thanks. I'll talk to you later."

I had a lot to think about. I understood what Frank was saying, but I also knew in my heart there were a lot of things that just weren't fair, and I didn't want to become a person who doesn't stand up for what I believe in, just to get a raise or keep the peace. How do you wrap a Mary Poppins attitude around what just doesn't feel right? What happens if you don't? Anger? Spending your life jaded? I spent a lot of time thinking about my experiences and the different conversations I had with Frank, but I was confused; my heart and ego were talking two different conversations.

The internal debate went on for quite some time, kind of like the cartoons: my everyday me in the middle, "the best me" on the left shoulder, and the "not-so best me" on the right shoulder. One side of me was saying, "Shannea, we've got to do better. Just try something different. Doing the same thing over and over again and expecting different results is insane. You can figure this out! Maybe Frank is right; he gets along because he chooses to get along. This isn't rocket science. You can make some changes to have different experiences if you choose to." Then there was the other side saying, "Man, forget Frank and everyone who thinks like him. You aren't some type of sellout! Aren't you tired of trying to bend over backwards and jump through hoops for other people? Why can't you just be yourself and that be enough? Aren't slavery and the 'yes'um' days over?"

My astrology sign is Libra. While I'm not sure exactly what I think about astrology, the justice scale is the symbol of Libra and I acknowledge I have a zeal for justice, equality, and fairness. Even as an adult, I've had a pretty tough time acclimating to the cliché that life isn't fair, even though many of my experiences clearly support the theory.

I think a common pitfall is the focus and preoccupation with being *right*. I'm not sure there is such a thing, and if there is, it might not be as black and white as we imagine it to be. What might seem *right* in one situation may not apply to the next, or what is *right* for you may not be *right* for me. Contrary to popular belief, right is really more subjective than most will admit, relative to the person judging and the objective.

So many times I've seen two people looking at the same thing and see something completely different. Perspective can vary for so many different reasons: the lens with which you see events, your morals, your current state of peace, and all the other dangers and traps of the human mind. If I could feel so right about something not that long ago that I am now beginning to see quite differently, and that is a change in perspective within the same me, it's a little comical that we think right should be so absolute.

I'm not sure how a person defines being right—is right synonymous with "my opinion?" If right is what you believe in—what supports your belief system, your personal rules of integrity—right, at best, can only mean what is *right for you.*

Could you imagine being a visitor in someone else's house and telling them how things should be done because *you* feel it is the right thing to do? My tolerance is low for what people think is the right thing for me to do on Webster Street! (That is the street where I live.) The short version is to take you and your *right*, right out of my space.

In order for someone to be right, someone usually has to be wrong. Do you know how hard it is to be successful, to be in a relationship, or to achieve a goal with someone you are labeling as being wrong? In most cases, as soon as you get into "right" and "wrong," you enter a power struggle that is often won by power and position with little consideration for "right," "wrong," or much else. Not all of the time, but a whole bunch of the time!

My point here is that I think there is a strong correlation between choosing to wag your tail and focusing more on being successful than being right. If you are aligning your actions with being successful, there can be an authentic peace and joy that emits a positive energy—tail wagging, if you will—because you feel good about what you are doing. How could you not feel good about what you're doing if you recognize your actions as your choices, and they are choices made in support of your success? Anything less than peace and joy should automatically be cause for you to make different choices.

The mind is a dangerous thing. People can make a cold argument for almost anything. I'm convinced you could create an argument that the moon is red if you choose. As I mentioned earlier, my conversation with Frank was the beginning of my transformation, but it took a while before I could really come to terms with changing my approach. Eventually I had another "aha moment." I think I just got tired of going through the same things, so I committed to taking control and working to have a different experience. I decided I was going to wag my tail! In my internal dialogue I asked myself questions like, "But why do you think dumbing it down a bit or showing yourself friendly is selling out? What does it really compromise? You talk to a child differently than you do adults to adjust to the level of learning and perspective; why would this be any different? Is it selling out, or effective communication?"

I started reading new books, rereading old books, and meditating, and I had a lot of conversations with people who seemed to be living a more peaceful successful life. I wanted to figure out where I was and what I really wanted. I made a list of the characteristics of the person I wanted to be and the life I wanted to live, and looked at the decisions I was making from day to day to see if they supported my goals. I thought about what I wanted, but I also thought about why I wanted it. I asked myself: what would I do if money weren't an object? If I could create my life with no holds barred, what would that look like?

I didn't have all of the answers, but I knew I wanted to get rid of the anger and live a life with more joy. I didn't want to crush others, and I definitely didn't want to be crushed. I didn't want to play the dog-eat-dog game. I wanted to have different experiences. I wanted to wag my tail.

Chapter 3
Learning to Wag My Tail

In choosing to wag my tail, I had to first wrap my mind around being successful in my objectives, and get away from my pride and being right. I think this is a lifelong process. In the beginning it was rough, and I weaved in and out of consciousness quite a bit. But as with most things, the more you work at it, the easier it becomes.

I did complete the recruit class to become a volunteer firefighter and served for a short while, but I gave up trying to become a career firefighter. I wish I could say it was all my choice, but the reality was the physical test was kicking my butt and I didn't want to keep my life in limbo. As far as volunteering, I was the only woman and only Brown person in my recruit class, and the only Brown person I ever saw in the entire department. In honor of the cliché "pick your battles," this was a battle I was willing to pass on.

Not passing the physical test is something I still struggle with. I may break news as the first sixty-year-old woman taking the physical test – just to know I can do it.

Through my fire fighting experience I also learned that a paramilitary structure may not be the best fit for someone attached to fair and right and wrong. I moved on to an industry I thought was more rooted in fairness and due process—human resources. Poor Shannea! So naive, so disillusioned!

I took a position as a human resources training associate. I knew pretty early on—probably in my interview, to be honest—that the other two people on my team, both of whom were considered my superiors, were messy women. I wanted the job because it paid more money than I was making, I thought it would be good for my career development, and most importantly, I felt I had to get out of my current job situation – yesterday! I was basically going from the skillet to the frying pan, but I made an argument for why it would work. I also thought I had enough experience in learning to wag my tail that I could give enough wags effortlessly to make it work and stay under the radar. Wrong!

I spoke to people every day, kept my opinion to myself for the most part, and tried to keep it moving. Unbeknownst to me, this group of people wanted much more than tail wagging—at least that is what it felt like. As far as the HR department, we were a team of three: the HR director, the HR manager, and me. Now, this title wackiness within a team of three should have been the first indicator there were some power and position issues. How do you have a manager and a director in a team of three? What are you managing and directing? The one person underneath you?

Shortly after I started, the director said to the manager, "I just don't think Shannea likes me! I see the way she is with you, and she doesn't joke and talk to me like she does you." She was right, too. I thought she was unstable as all get out, so I tried to keep my distance: speak, slip in a joke or two, and move on!

The manager and the director were tight. They would sit in the director's office and gossip and laugh (ridiculous loud laughs, falling out of the seat, slappin' the desk and the whole nine yards). It was like the middle school clique where if you didn't join in talking about people, you could be ousted. Once I had a conversation with the manager about the director, how she could throw a person under the bus or keep them in good graces, all depending on how she was feeling. In that conversation, the manager disclosed how she didn't trust the director, thought she was a little scandalous, didn't like her very much, and felt she wasn't very bright. I said, "Wow! I never would have guessed that from the way you interact with her."

The manager said, "She is someone who needs a lot of attention, so I kiss her butt and talk about people with her because it keeps it cool. I've never made as much money as I make now, and compared to the job I left, I can manage her." Ah, she was wagging her tail! Now for me, I felt like I couldn't do what the manager was doing. Talking about people, engaging in some business practices that I had issues with just to keep the peace as long as it wasn't happening to me—that was a price I wasn't willing to pay. The manager, she felt it was a concession she could easily make to support her family and her career path—choice!

I didn't care much for either one of them and definitely couldn't trust either of them any further than I could throw them, but I thought, 'okay, I can wag my tail here. I can show myself friendly. I can accept what is so and focus on my objective and concentrate on being successful rather than passing judgment.' Even though I felt the manager was a little immature and I was surprised about some of her choices, I genuinely could connect with her as a person and appreciate where she was in her life journey. I wagged my tail for the manager, and the manager wagged her tail for the director; not ideal for the long haul, but doable as opposed to unemployment. To take things back to that "if you choose to walk in the water, don't complain about being wet" analogy: I knew I didn't like the water, but instead of flailing around, splashing, and making it harder to swim for myself and those around me, I thought to focus on an exit strategy out of the water. I would honor my choice while I chose to walk in the water.

I managed to dodge most of the bullets and wag my tail enough to get by for a few months. Boy, dog poo definitely rolls downhill! I made the least, financially, of the three of us, but you best believe I did most of the work. There were some rough pockets, but I had a plan and worked hard to stay centered. I knew there were some positive things about my position that I could use as a stepping stone in my career path. And as I said before, I was making more money than I had in a long time, and I had a lot of flexibility in my schedule.

I started studying for my human resources certification and started the blue print to my way out. Success in this particular situation was first, staying employed until I wanted to leave so there would be no interruption in my income, and second, to find a more ideal situation so I wouldn't be going from the skillet to the frying pan once again.

One of the lessons I was learning was the detriment that can come from making decisions from an unfocused place and living in crisis management. When you are drowning, it is not the time to buy a boat! Anytime you make a decision from a crisis management standpoint, it is probable you will miss vital information and not make sound decisions. Remember, there were warning signs during my interview, but instead of focusing on my ultimate purpose and long-term goals, I had tunnel vision about trying to get out of my current position. I can try to defend my decision to take the new position by saying I didn't know it was as bad as it was, which is true, but I think two things happened: one, I was so desperate to get in a different situation I downplayed the warning signs, and two, I overestimated my own skill set. At that point I had embraced wagging my tail, but I don't think I had fully grasped everything Frank had said. I thought of tail wagging more to just get by or a means to an end rather than authentic peace and joy that creates pure satisfaction, which is probably why it only lasted for a few months.

So I had a plan and everything was cool, until I pissed off the manager! The manager stopped being so eager to serve as the buffer between me and the director. If I thought dog poo rolled downhill before, I was in no way prepared for the deluge of poo that followed when I was out of the manager's good graces.

Long story short, both the manager and the director started piling on work like nobody's business. In addition to the work load, I was written up for something that happened over a month earlier. I don't remember exactly what the write-up said, but it had something to do with a procedure the manager told me to implement. One of the venue managers at the company—and the managers had quite a bit of clout, especially if they managed one of the venues that brought in a lot of revenue—didn't like the policy the manager asked me to implement because it affected how he could staff his team; he laid in on the director big time. The director in turn laid in on me, even though I was following a directive from my supervisor, and had the email to prove it. Now we were getting into the tricks of reporting to more than one person, and he said she said, with no backing from my manager. Of course the manager did not stand up for me. She stated that yes, she gave me the directive, but only as a scare tactic to the venue managers, and that she didn't actually mean for me to apply the it. Say what?

I spent a lot of time talking to Frank and trying to stay centered. I reminded myself to focus on being successful with no complaints—just focus on how to get out of the water, which would equate to success. While continuing to work, I started networking and searching for other career opportunities, and applied a lot of focus and energy on tightening up my plan. It wasn't easy, but it was a lot easier than it had been in the past. One of the challenges with initially working to wag my tail was trying to remember that I was doing it for me, to be successful in my objectives, and not for them. When I thought about doing it for them, my ego and pride would feel challenged and the internal debate would resurface. The thought of doing it for them solicited thoughts of being a sellout, being a house Negro, and a bunch of thoughts that made the internal conflict resurface. When I thought about doing it for me, when I thought about not complaining and instead finding a way to get out of the water, it generated a completely different energy from within. What were once viewed as painful kiss-butt actions now turned into small victories and stepping stones to support my master plan—and, ultimately, a better, stronger me.

When I was written up, I was furious—hot as fish grease! I talked to Frank about how to respond. I wanted to respond by putting in writing how bogus the accusations were, and submit some facts about their activities on record. I had the directive from the manager in writing in an email, minus any of her supposed "scare tactic only" verbiage, and other documentation I felt undermined the write-up. Frank stopped me dead in my tracks and asked me what my intentions were, what I planned to accomplish if I did that, and most importantly, what I thought would be the outcome. Frank bottom-lined everything by asking what my objective was, what I wanted to get from the situation, and what the probable outcome was based on how I was planning to respond. I told him I thought they would more than likely get defensive and fire me if I responded the way I was thinking. He asked me if I wanted to get fired. When I said no, he asked me why I would make a choice that didn't support success—the outcome I wanted. I answered that, while I didn't want to get fired, I felt being fired was inevitable and that I knew the unemployment process and this write-up, and my response, would come into question.

Frank said, "Are you planning for unemployment or are you planning for success? If success is using this job as a stepping stone and headway into the rest of your plans, why would you take actions that would support your worst-case scenario instead of your objective? Why take actions that enroll in a game that will most likely end up in unemployment? It's almost as if you have lost the will of choice and conceded to unemployment being the inevitable, and I see a lot of other options."

Silenced again! I didn't respond to the write-up, and turned up my intensity: my intensity with finding my exit strategy and wagging my tail. Normally I would have written some lawyer-type statement that would be a great defense, and cop the coldest attitude to go with it. Sort of like a return serve daring them to hit the ball back again. The problem is that there usually is a return hit. It's not like I've ever turned on my funky attitude and had an employer respond by saying, "Okay, okay, okay! Don't be mad at us, Shannea, we're sorry and we take back the write-up." Instead of doing what I would have done in the past, I responded very cordially, as if it didn't happen. I spoke even more frequently, told myself jokes before walking in the office so I would be smiling a genuine smile, and asked questions I knew the answer to in an effort to be more interactive and hand over the power for which they were struggling. In essence, I was buying myself more time and a more peaceful environment—a cleaner pool of water to walk in—while I was there. It was completely new for me, and totally against what they were expecting. I found out through the grapevine after the fact that the director had decided to give me three days from the write-up to make changes visible to her or else I was out. To her surprise, and quite frankly mine as well, I did the opposite of what she was expecting me to do. The director fully expected the write-up to serve to bait me to bite so it would be an easily justifiable termination. By making a choice to respond positively and not enroll I not only dodged the bullet, but perhaps the crucifixion!

So, while I had been successful for a while, when it got a little thick the true colors came out—theirs and mine. Even though I had begun my paradigm shift and was committed to wagging my tail, I still had a lot of work to do, and I still was missing a few crucial pieces to the puzzle. It's like if you have infidelity issues in your marriage. You say you will no longer cheat, but you still put yourself in vulnerable situations, using justifications and sayings like, "There is nothing wrong with looking and having friends." The choices you are making don't support what you say you are committed to. You may not be actively cheating, but your heart hasn't changed. In my case, I smiled more and tried to engage in more small talk and let a lot of small things go without putting up a fuss, but I still felt a separation between me and my co-workers, and I didn't genuinely want to be in relationship with them. I just wanted to make it well enough to get by. I changed what I communicated outwardly, but in my head I felt it was a company full of scandalous ding-dongs.

When my relationship with the manager changed, she not only stopped serving as a buffer between me and the director; she joined forces with the director. It got to the point where I was near tears. They doubled my work load and started creating timelines for me to complete new tasks—a part of the game I had never experienced with this company. Some of the flexibility I had was taken away, and there were hints dropped about whether or not I would get some of the compensation promised to me. The tipping point was when I was given a project assigned to the director. She was given two months to complete the project. She passed the project on to me after her deadline had passed and gave me one week to complete the project. She refused to remove or push back any of my regular work. Then the director and the manager took the day off. I went to the parking lot and called Frank in tears.

At this point I had been on a few job interviews and made some good connections. When you are learning and trying to implement new behavior, it is tough sometimes. While I was committed to wagging my tail and approaching things differently, we still had thirty some-odd years of background story to override. It was like being on a diet where my goal was to lose fifty pounds and I had lost forty, but hit a plateau and the chocolate mousse pie started calling me. I felt like I was wagging my tail and was committed to being successful, but it wasn't keeping the power players from trying to step on my neck. When I hit this wall I felt like I couldn't take it anymore. I said to Frank, while crying, "I'm just mad! I already know all the stuff, but I need help trying to remember it. I'm just so mad. I know there is no such thing as fair, but man! It just seems like sometimes the harder I try, the thicker it gets. What about me? When do I get some justice? I'm tired and I'm mad. I'm just mad!"

He asked me what was going on and I told him about the new work assignment and the work load. I told him I felt like they were pushing my back against the wall, trying to make me quit. When I would pass one test, they would turn it up and add a few new tests. Frank kindly listened to me cry and vent, and, when I was finished, asked me what was my reason for being there; what was success in terms of that situation, and how would I reach success? He asked me point-blank, "Whatever it is they've asked you to do, can you do it?"

I said yes I could do it, but talked about how long it would take me to do it, the hardship it would create for me, blah blah blah.

Frank bottom lined me again, saying, "So you *can* do what they are asking you to do?"

"Yes, but it isn't reasonable or fair and I don't want to; I don't want to restructure everything I have going on to do this. I don't want this job to consume me like that."

Frank said, "Okay, then don't! Don't do it."

"But I have…Okay. I get it."

By the end of the conversation I had renewed my commitment to my objective, was laughing, and had wrapped my mind back around being successful. I walked back in to my office and said out loud, to myself and any of my eavesdropping harassers, "Take two!" Just saying that out loud, made me laugh. I just started chipping away at the craziness laid out for me. Within five minutes of parking my behind back in my chair, Frank called me and said he had just received a call from one of the companies I had interviewed with. Later that morning, I also got a call and subsequently a much better job offer with a $4,000 sign-on bonus. Within the next two weeks I received at least two additional job offers, one with an almost doubled sign-on bonus than the first company offered, better opportunity and benefits, and a much higher salary.

I wholeheartedly believe that my experience came full circle because of choice. In that experience I had to constantly reach in and tie a new knot when I felt like my life line was slipping. Once I let go of the energy I had been wasting on resistance, I was able to focus on positive output—and create room for positive energy and experiences to come to me.

You have to know what success is for you, and then every day commit to being successful and making choices that support your goals and your commitment. I think my attitude—my tail wagging if you will—was instrumental in new doors opening. I promise, no exaggeration, in the interview cycle that came from working to leave that company, I had the best interview experience I have ever had. I know that the peace and joy I was centered in and committed to made the difference. The company I ended up signing with offered me $11,000 more than I was making at the time, a $7,000 sign-on bonus paid up front in full, and stock units worth $40,000. I asked the hiring manager why she hired me over the other candidates. She said, "Shannea, I knew within five minutes of talking to you, 'she's it!'" She said, "We had been interviewing for months, and I was committed to taking as long as it takes to find the right fit. As soon as I sat and started talking to you, I knew you were what I wanted. You had the technical skill set and background experience, but it was your personality. I knew you were a people person. I knew you were someone who gets it. I knew you were someone totally connected to customer service and giving people the best possible experience."

Wow! I was floored. I felt like I had won. While I was happy about the job opportunity and felt I had made a major upgrade, my victory was in the personal growth. I felt I had triumphed and hadn't let the manager and director crush my spirit—that I hadn't let the adversity stop me from being my best self and creating the life I wanted to live, that I was being progressive and growing as a person. But wait: it gets better!

I gave the director and manager my two week notice. I had to have a little talk with myself to resist wanting to stick it to them and leave them with work piled high. I reminded myself of the life I wanted to live, what I was committed to, and—let's not fool with dear old karma. I gave a nice resignation letter, short and to the point—"I'm moving on, thank you for the experience and opportunity." That week, the director and manager asked me to step into the director's office and told me they were letting me go now, before my full two weeks. No continued pay, no extended benefits; get my stuff and hand over my keys!

I won't get into all of the specifics, but rest assured, good did prevail. Several months after leaving I pursued action against the early termination and possible retaliation, and I was compensated satisfactorily. I'm sure, once again, it was a direct reflection on the way I chose to respond, both in attitude and action. My immediate response to the director and manager was a simple, "Okay," instead of arguing or engaging in an exchange that wouldn't have been effective in the moment. And of course I left to go see Frank—I needed an in-person visit for that one!

I did two things differently: one, I stayed present and focused on the big picture and centered myself in all that I had to be thankful for. Two, I used the extra time I gained from the early separation to take care of myself and offer myself the balance I knew I needed to be my best (massage and great dates with friends – yeah!). And three, I put the separation in my mental rolodex with a flag to do something progressive in my response and not be a victim. I was immediately satisfied with what was so, *and* committed to doing something about it. It wasn't an "either/or." It was "and/both." I accept this (no resistance) *and* I'm going to do something about it. You really can do both. I think sometimes we think anger should bear witness to our intensity or passion about change, and I just don't think it has to be that way. I was so excited about the life I was experiencing and the doors that were opening, I didn't spend any energy on resisting the director and the manager. Even in that moment, the pettiness and energy from the manager and director seemed so yesterday.

A seamless learning experience? Absolutely not! And there is continued learning to date. No one is one hundred percent all of the time—no, not one. But the initial commitment to wagging my tail, coupled with constantly recommitting and implementing the learning, has proven a pivotal paradigm shift.

Chapter 4
When They Throw Rocks at the Dog

Growl but don't bite

A couple of years after that tail-wagging conversation with Frank, I was working for a start-up technology company. The experience was kicking my butt. Despite everything I tried to do to wag my tail and show myself friendly, I felt like I was getting slammed. My position was office manager, and I reported to the vice president of operations—the top position of our Seattle branch. He and I got along great, but the office manager in our corporate office in

Nashville, Tennessee was a serious thorn in my side. I would make decisions and work through situations where our team members needed assistance. She would call me and question each decision I made, in the end saying, "Oh! Okay! Well, I was just checking." She asked to be included in correspondence to team members just to be kept abreast of what was going on. I'd include her, and then she would contact the person directly and ask them to work through her. She was in an office in Nashville, Tennessee, and I was within spitting distance, but she *needed* to be involved.

I called her one morning when there weren't any particular issues to address to have a conversation about our communication, how we could set things up so we weren't both working on the same issues, and, how to encourage the Seattle office to use me as a resource to support our team building—the human resources way of asking 'what is going to take to get you to butt out and stop undermining me?' Her response to that conversation was, "Who put you up to this?"

I was especially frustrated one day and I called Frank. I hadn't spoken to him in months.

"This is Frank," he answered.

The first thing that exploded out of my mouth was, "What do you do if they throw rocks at the dog?"

Remembering our initial dog analogy conversation, once again Frank started cracking up laughing. Now mind you, I hadn't talked to Frank in months, but that is the kind of relationship we have. We go hard when we are active in our relationship, but we are not the kind of friends that necessarily talk every day—or every week, for that matter. Needless to say, as soon as I said those words, he not only knew who I was, but he knew exactly what I was talking about.

Through his laughter Frank managed to spit out, "Well, what do you mean, 'what if they throw rocks at the dog?' What is happening?"

"Well, I'm working hard to wag my tail. I've gotten past my *right* and *wrong* and I'm pulling all kinds of tricks out my hat, even balancing doggy biscuits on my nose! I'm wagging my tail all over the place, but they're killing me! It is like they are literally throwing rocks at the dog. It is almost as if by wagging my tail, it is getting worse instead of better! I feel like the softer I come and make concessions to try to make it work, the more they try to run over me. At least when people claimed to be intimidated, I didn't have people pushing me!"

"I see what you're saying," Frank replied. "Well, if they're throwing rocks at the dog, maybe you need to show a little teeth, and even growl a little bit. Just don't bite anybody!"

Now I was cracking up laughing, which was a great thing for a couple of reasons. First, the meekness of the moment created a safe place for vulnerability, consciousness, and warmth to help me get back on track. Second, and what I think is the coolest thing about analogies, what started out as a cry for help and me slipping back into my victim stance was once again equated to something not personal—just the stuff in a situation!

Frank continued saying, "Just don't bite anybody! Cause you know what they do to dogs that bite, don't you?"

I started laughing and answered, "They put them to sleep!"

Frank said, "That's right, and in this case, putting you to sleep will be firing you, changing the terms of the deal, or doing something else to get you out of there."

Here is what I want to point out about this moment. This is what is true about both the analogy and people. When people act out, when dogs bite, when there is a person or something that people can easily attach to a "wrong," the "why" of the story is often minimized or omitted with highlights on the isolation of the action to support judgment of the wrong. Rarely do you hear the background stories about what provoked the situation.

When you have a person at their job that gets nitpicked to death, passed up for promotion, written up because they are at the mercy of some egotistical person who is in a bad place in their life, there is no media coverage of the company and the experiences of this person—just that they snapped. I'm not justifying the action; I just think ignoring the igniters helps dismiss accountability and some of the root causes that allow some abuse to continue to perpetuate.

My point is, people don't focus or choose to remember so much the cause and effect, just the end result. So if you bite, or choose not to wag your tail, or do anything else that stands in the way of your success, you have to stand up and have a real live conversation with yourself and own those choices. If you choose to be *right* and can deal with the consequences of your choices, okay. If you choose to make some concessions, not worry about some things, let a few rocks go by, and wag your tail to be successful, same message: okay! If you equate success to balance, some type of combination of the two extremes: same message. Because people have different tolerance levels and different objectives, we may respond to situations differently. Something that sticks out and bothers you may not even register on my radar.

At the end of the day it all amounts to your choices. It is always your choice. If you own the choice, equally own the consequences, but know you always have a choice. Everybody has their own boundary lines, what they will and won't do, just as I imagine dogs have different thresholds for when they bite. Some dogs bite on sight, some dogs only bite when provoked, and some dogs don't bite even when abused. Of course I'm hoping you choose success that gives you optimal peace and positively contributes to the universe.

Chapter 5
Why I Wag My Tail

I want to point out that for me—for me Shannea, in my experience—there is a huge difference in embracing the thought of wagging your tail and choosing to prefer success over being right, and the willingness to do anything to get what you want—to be unscrupulous. Choosing to wag your tail isn't some slick way of validating being a scoundrel and dismissing cause and effect, or the consequences of choices you make. To even begin to embrace the concept of choosing success over being right or wagging your tail, you have to first identify what success is for you and your parameters. Only you can decide what success is for you, and what you are willing to pay.

When you are making choices to support your objectives and take full responsibility for your choices, you have a different experience with the universe. When you transition from a victim mentality to a position of power—power over you, the life you create and your contribution to your world—there is peace and joy that comes from that position.

I had a woman say to me once, "I don't know, Shannea. You do good work, but you don't say good morning to me or talk to me unless I say something first. If I ask you a question, you will answer the question, but nothing more or nothing less." This particular conversation took place within one month of a work project with a new company where I focused my energy on the technical aspects of my responsibilities—the stuff listed in the job description. What I failed to realize is that, in the project I was approaching, the team I was working with needed soft skills probably ten times more than my technical skills; it just wasn't recognized enough to be listed as a priority in the job description.

To paraphrase, this woman was saying, 'yeah, you do great work, but I want to have *a good experience with you! I want to chit-chat with you in the morning, see how your weekend went, and feel warm and fuzzy after interacting with you.'*

That was tough for me; that wasn't what I signed up for. I didn't take the position in hopes of making new friends. I strongly felt that her sense of entitlement was to have me make her feel good, and she was not entitled to that—that's extra. If it comes naturally, cool, but if not—oh well! I don't go home upset because someone didn't say hi to me or share their personal story. As long as you aren't doing anything to prevent me from getting my work done, we don't have a problem. Then something happened!

One day while driving home I was analyzing what I assessed as this whole sense of entitlement, and reflected on the feedback from the woman. I thought, why do some people feel it is their right to have people suck up to them? Why isn't it enough just to do a good job? When I was self-employed, did I feel that way about my employees? Is it a white thing or a power thing? I had worked for a Brown woman who clearly expected a lot of bowing down from all of her staff, her husband included, so I had some experience that encouraged me to take my questions and analyzing beyond race. But I still couldn't pinpoint the energy. If I hire someone to cut my grass, is it enough for them to cut my grass or do I unconsciously want a bunch of extras?

Out of nowhere, it hit me!

If I have two gardeners that perform close to the same level of work but have two different social approaches, would it make a difference? I have Gardener A, who while in the yard working when I come home says, "Hey Shannea! How was your day today? Anything new going on?" Then I have Gardener B, who is startled when I come in my gate, looks up, kind of waves, and will answer any question and respond to me, but has a disposition that expresses a preference not to talk to me unless it is yard related. While the technical skills—the actual yard work—may not differ very much, there is a distinct difference in the experience I would have with the two gardeners.

While I was thinking about this I cracked myself up because I was getting an attitude just glossing over the analogy—my yard, my money, and you feel like it is a strain just to speak to me? So in this light bulb moment I recognize I have the same sense of entitlement that I have been persecuting others for. I hired services for just my yard, but there is a soft skill, an expectation based on my interpretation of appropriateness that I innately felt should apply. Yes, I hired you to take care of the lawn, but why wouldn't you speak on general principle? Now, even in that hypothetical situation, I would be surprised to see myself pushing my way into someone's personal space, and I definitely don't see myself letting someone go because they want to keep to their self, especially if there is no issue with their work. But what I do recognize and can relate to as the bigger point for me, is that, given the choice, I would choose a more warm and personal experience, even in a business context.

So now we have the ultimate challenge, Shannea challenging Shannea: my best self challenging my everyday self! So, Miss Shannea! When it is your dollar, your power, and your money, you want the best service, but you also want some simple courtesies to make the experience more pleasant. So why do you feel it is so undeserving from your employer, or those you work with? When you think about a company you own, or a person you pay to maintain your yard, you want good work, *but also a pleasant experience.* Yet, when it comes to you, your focus has been on delivering an excellent work product with little attention to your co-workers having a pleasant experience. *You* have a sense of entitlement to be left alone as long as your work is stellar. Maybe the "sucking up," as you call it, isn't added in the job description because what you call sucking up is common courtesy that others feel is a no-brainer and should come without mention in everyday experience.

Now, don't get me wrong; I could write a few more books addressing some of the everyday injustices and cause-and-effect that make it more difficult to extend common courtesies. But here, I'm addressing my output and my responsibilities. We've all heard the clichés that speak to not being able to control a situation but controlling how we respond. I'm saying, in my experience, in my journey to learn to wag my tail from an authentic place of joy, I think there is a lot of truth to owning your part and your response.

I still have boundaries and lines I'm not willing to cross, but I equally believe that one of the common denominators in human beings is that most of us desire to have pleasurable experiences that are attainable at a level where you can maintain your personal integrity and your boundaries; something along the lines of "just being nice!" There is a way to say no, and there is a way to say H, E, double hockey sticks, friggin' no, with extra emphasis. Maybe sometimes people (myself included here) get so caught up in saying no and being right that they forget they are dealing with a person, a person who equally has their own life journey they're trying to figure out; that there is a way to state the 'no,' but be conscious of life while sharing your perspective (being successful). You can set boundaries without crushing people.

In all actuality, I think if people had to choose, most would choose mediocre work over great work that comes with a bad attitude. I don't know how many times I've taken an extra thirty minutes to look something up rather than deal with someone whom I feel is a jerk that could give me the answer in thirty seconds. As a business owner, I wouldn't hire a person who has a wealth of information if the person was unapproachable. What good is information if it can't be utilized? That's like having a high tech computer and no power cord!

I have an ex-boyfriend who isn't the brightest bulb in the bunch, and is more on the lazy side when it comes to work ethic. The people at his job love this man. They have given him cars, floor seats to basketball games, invites to fancy events held by some of the company executives, all types of perks. While he was getting Grade-A treatment, I was struggling to keep work assignments. My ex-boyfriend's company has tried to motivate him and give him opportunities to advance—"Here's an open door opportunity; what do you want to do? Show us what you want, and we'll help you get it! Is there any training we can pay to put you through? Do you have any interest in any particular function?" If the invitation wasn't about partying, fun and games, he would oh-so-graciously decline!

So you have a person who is probably not the best worker on the technical or output end, not very motivated, not innovative or creative, but a person almost everyone knows and wants to have around. While I, on the other hand, received great praise for my work and kicked butt on my projects, it's safe to say people weren't dying to have me around. The significance in the difference? They love him! He wags his tail effortlessly and authentically!

I have a friend I went to high school with who is making around $85,000 a year with no college education or technical certification. She works in a management position and was recently asked—didn't apply, but was asked—to work for a division within her company that most people would sell tail to get into. They asked her! Now, don't get me wrong; she has a host of experience and on the job training, and she is definitely someone you want on your team as far as brain power. But I think they chose her first for her soft skills, and secondly for her technical experience. A woman on the team that propositioned her worked with her on a project and observed her customer service, the way she responds to pressure, and the way she treats the people around her and told her boss they should ask her to join their team. Part of her welcome wagon was a trip to Tahoe—of course, on them.

Do you hear what I'm saying, people? It took a lonnngggg time for me to get the message that your soft skills are just as important as your technical skills, if not more so. There is a saying: "People will forget what you said, people will forget what you did, but they will remember how you made them feel." I couldn't agree more.

When I've started a new experience with an organization, either as an employee, visitor or consultant, what I hear more than anything when getting the introductory walk around are comments like: 'he's the nicest person you'll ever meet,' 'she's a true gem,' 'we just love her.' Rarely, and I do mean rarely, do I hear in the initial greeting comments about skill level and work ethic. The comments I hear most frequently are made based on the interactive experiences. Later, after delving into the work product, the technical skills come into play. But the initial sound bites are all about character and soft skills.

It may have taken a long time, but once I got it, it became incredibly important to me to leave people with good experiences after our interactions. Even when I deal with someone whom I consider "not user friendly," I still want to honor my commitment to myself and my universe, and make a positive contribution.

I think some of our old fashioned values—customer service, respect and loyalty—have taken a back seat to our technological advances. I see the emphasis our society places on innovation, creativity, and the new best thing, and I see how I unconsciously became a product of my environment. In my frustration and exhaustion from being on the short side of the "fair" stick, I justified my own behavior and focused on developing my technical skills as a coping mechanism— so I'd have more tools to stomp with the big dogs in an effort to join the tail chase of innovation, and placing product over people. It happened so subtly that I didn't realize I wasn't succeeding because I was playing a game foreign to my heart.

While I was volunteering as a Senior Cadet with a fire department, one of the lieutenants pulled me aside and asked me, "Why are you trying to just blend in instead of being the leader we all know you to truly be?"

I responded with a genuinely puzzled, "Say what?"

She said, "I'm serious, Shannea. You try not to answer questions or direct people, and you just do your part, but the team members keep coming to you naturally because they see it—they know you know the answers, and they like the way you engage. You see people like Smitz? She's begging for the spotlight and constantly trying to lead, and they keep coming to you anyway. Your teammates see it, and so do we, so what is your problem?"

I said, "I'm tired of the work it takes to lead, and I do that in every other capacity in my life. I made it my mission to come here and just exist—to try to take care of myself, for once, and not everyone else."

She said, "Okay. You can try to avoid it if you want, but I don't think you will genuinely be happy, and I think you are doing a disservice to yourself and your team. Shannea, the great leaders don't lead from a power of expertise, they lead from the power of connecting to people, and that is what differentiates them from other leaders. Not everyone has it, but you do."

Obviously it took me a lot longer to see some of what Frank and my lieutenant saw long before I made my connection. And they both are right. I choose to wag my tail because of my heart, the life experiences I want to have, the level of peace I choose to experience, my calling, my life purpose, and the desire to be connected to people and my universe and experience interdependence, because of the God that lives in me. If my purpose is to help people be their best selves, there is no way I can minimize the importance of connecting. Whenever there is a disconnect for any reason—when people are afraid of me, intimidated by me, or responding to a stereotype of me—chances are that disconnect emits negative energy to all parties involved. If I can do something about it in those instances, I want to. If you could wag your tail and get someone to put their dukes down, why wouldn't you? I choose to wag my tail because despite the differences, there are similarities that make the differences pale in comparison. I wag my tail because I don't want to be a victim of my own living, or lack of living. I wag my tail because even though I can't change everything, I feel good about the things I can, and that change is what I'm committed to.

If the bottom line is that there is a commitment I want to honor, a purpose I feel I am meant to serve, and a life experience I want to have, it isn't enough to be dismissive on the level of cause and effect. It isn't enough for me to live a life less than the one I choose just because of the external factors—because of what other people are doing to me, themselves, and our environment. People can treat me a certain way because of how they perceive me, but what about my choice? I get to choose how I respond to them, and either continue to perpetuate the madness, or break the chain.

Even if you are a person who feels that being your best self, putting out good energy, and having optimal experiences is a bunch of crap, let's take it to a basement boogie level. How many times have you gone above and beyond what you are required to do to help someone who is a jerk? How many times have you had someone go out of their way for you or deliver excellent service—an experience that lingers in your mind and made you smile for a while—while you were being a jerk?

Let's take Kobe Bryant for example: some argue he is one of the best to every play the game of basketball, but boy have there been some issues—and mostly around his soft skills, or lack thereof. In the beginning of his career there were a lot of issues because Kobe didn't want to hang with the fellas. After a game, Kobe's idea of a good time was reviewing the game tape to perfect his craft. Just like I thought early in my career that great work ethics and Grade-A work product would take me far, Kobe thought it was all about the game. What is crazy is, in a black and white logical world, you naturally question: 'why isn't the game of basketball all about the game?' 'Why isn't great work enough?' Because both work and basketball are done by people, and people aren't just black and white and logical; there is emotion and spirit and ego and a host of other elements that contribute to who we are and how we operate.

Authentic peace

Some people I have shared my tail wagging analogy with have thought the synopsis is that "you do what you have to do to get what you want." Well, kind of, but there is a bigger point. It's more like you make choices to support the life you want—not chase an "it" or one particular thing, but the big picture: what you ultimately want. A dog doesn't wag its tail on command or *just* for a treat. I'm still far from a dog expert, but I'm guessing there aren't many instances where a dog is wagging its tail with an ulterior motive to "have a little human din din!" When a dog wags its tail it is usually authentically indicative of a peaceful, approachable disposition. The general thought is if the dog is wagging its tail, the dog is cool and it is okay to approach or pet the dog.

I don't think you wag your tail to play a game, or *just* to get a raise or a promotion, or any other means to an end. There are many people who try. Often it is transparent, at least to some, or comes with consequences for being disingenuous—or, if nothing else, I'll say it again: good old karma!

The conversation with Frank definitely was the start of a long journey. To sustain the travel has taken a paradigm shift in my thinking, constant effort, and dedication. Frank or anyone else couldn't have just told me to wag my tail; I had to get some reasoning and sense of purpose with it for myself, in my head and in my heart.

My journey and commitment to living my best life and supporting and encouraging others to live theirs takes constant focus, dedication and recommitting; but since I've begun this journey, my life has changed for the better. There are things I still struggle with, things I've thought I've mastered until an experience proves that to be untrue. But both personally and professionally, I have relationships and experiences that provide a level of peace I spent a lot of time trying to find in other things: religion, relationships, family and sometimes even seclusion. But in all of the external things I sought, nothing changed until I searched my own heart.

I recently starting working for a new company. On my first day I hugged one of my co-workers—or she may have hugged me; I'm not sure. As soon as we saw each other, both of our arms flew open and we embraced in a hug so tight you would have thought we were long lost friends. This is a woman I had only seen on two other occasions: my interviews for the position. We muttered out something about being so happy to see each other, and I'm telling you, you wouldn't have been able to slap the smiles off our faces. Now I have experiences like that all of the time. The company I left didn't want me to go, and we had a day full of hugs and "I'm going to miss you" exchanges. I'm going to the holiday party for the company I left in a few weeks! Now, even when I'm not looking for a job, I get job offers, business partnering proposals, and other offers to be in relationship in some capacity. I even get requests to "just keep me up-to-date with what you are doing because you are one to watch!" I mention that only to stress the difference the journey has made. I've made marginal changes in my technical skills, but a huge change in heart!

When people are afraid, or dealing with something new or unfamiliar, it is easy to slip into either role of the dog analogy – either the person afraid of the dog behaving based on fear, or the dog reacting to the abuse of behavior generated by fear. I hope in sharing my journey, sharing why and how I came to wag my tail, it motivates self-reflection and authentic tail wagging for you. May you wag indefinitely!

Afterword

The process of getting this book in print has put more hair on my chest than I ever would have imagined. I have experienced more personal hurt and disappointment than I thought possible at this juncture in my life.

There are moments where I have questioned continuing with production. Some mornings I look in the mirror at my swollen eyes from days of crying, struggle with basic functions and wonder if I even have a tail any more—let alone if it's wagging. When I am struggling, I question if I'm fit to write my own words. Feelings of regressing, failure in relationships, and being a hypocrite cloud my head.

Yes, I hurt, I cry, I don't understand some things, I get angry, I suffer loss, I disappoint others, I'm disappointed by others, I wish things were different, I make mistakes – but in the midst of all of that, I still wag my tail! What I know, even on the foggy mornings – what I know, even with all of the ups and downs – what I know, is that I not only wag my tail, but the "ups" in my life 100% come from wagging my tail and I love it. While it is hard sometimes, being committed to good love in and good love out actually makes life easier. I am clear on my commitment, my purpose, and why I am here on this earth.

Living your best life doesn't mean you will be perfect or fall no more. It just means you may fall less often and when you do fall it might be easier to get back up.

2975050

Made in the USA